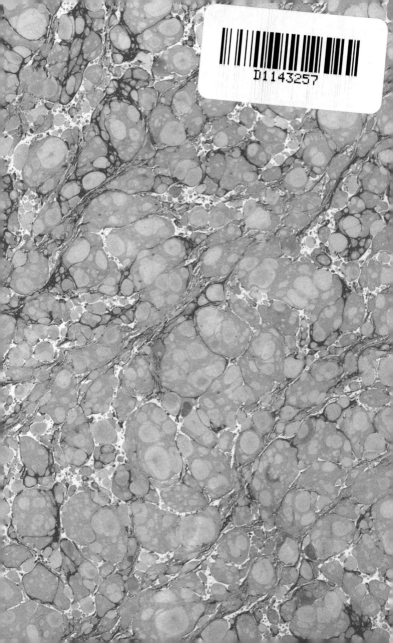

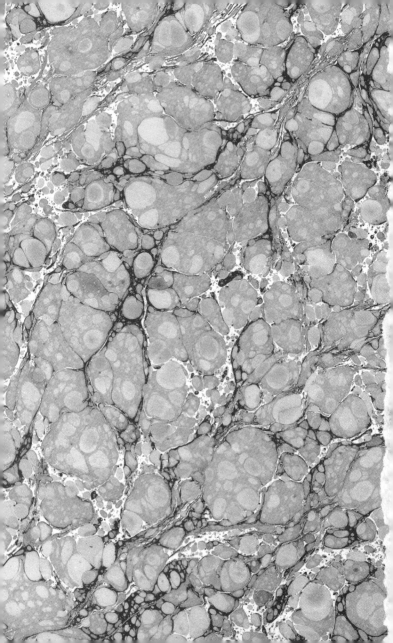

SIR WALTER'S WIT & WISDOM

SIR WALTER'S
WIT &
WISDOM

COMPILED BY
ERIC ANDERSON

THE
ABBOTSFORD
PRESS
2013

This collection
first published in 2013 by
THE ABBOTSFORD PRESS
Melrose · Roxburghshire · Scotland TD6 9BQ

Designed and typeset in Verdigris by Dalrymple
Printed and bound in Poland by OZGraf

ISBN 978 0 9575205 0 9

Cover: Sir Henry Raeburn (1756–1823)
Portrait of Sir Walter Scott, 1808 (detail)
*By kind permission of the Duke of Buccleuch
& Queensberry KBE*
Frontispiece: Augustin Edouart (1789–1861)
*Silhouette of Sir Walter Scott, c.*1830

INTRODUCTION

 HEN SIR WALTER SCOTT died in 1832 he was mourned as a great man as well as a great writer. The tragedy of his final years was regarded as a story as heroic and remarkable as anything in his fiction. Seven years earlier, at the age of fifty-four and at the peak of his powers and his popularity, he had been ruined by the sudden bankruptcy of his publisher and his printer. By the laws of the time he was responsible, as a partner in the printing business, for the debts of both firms. Instead of declaring himself bankrupt and restoring his fortunes within a few years by his writing, he resolved that no-one should lose a penny if he could help it. He set about clearing the debt with his pen and thanks to his heroic exertions half of it was repaid before his death and the remainder by the sale of his copyrights.

For more than twenty years he had been the world's most popular novelist. His twenty-six novels

– *Waverley. Guy Mannering, Rob Roy, Ivanhoe* and the rest – and narrative poems like *The Lay of the Last Minstrel, Marmion* and *The Lady of the Lake* were translated into most European languages and read throughout the civilized world. They remained best-sellers for a hundred years after his death. In America and Britain only Shakespeare and the Bible were read by more people.

His influence on world literature was immense. The Waverley Novels were unlike any that had gone before. In effect Scott invented the historical novel where (as in Shakespeare's history plays) fictional characters take part in real historical events alongside characters from history. *War and Peace, The Hunchback of Notre Dame, Vanity Fair* and the historical novels in vogue today were all inspired by Scott's example.

Scott also introduced Scotland to the world. Until his poems and novels became all the rage, the country was almost unknown to the rest of Europe. It was Scott who popularized the image of Scotland as a place of history and romance, of wild scenery, colourful tartans and brave and honourable clansmen. Whether they know it or not the tens of thousands of tourists who visit Scotland each year have been drawn there by Walter Scott.

Famous for his narrative poems and for the novels which almost everyone suspected to be his (they were published anonymously until he admitted authorship at the time of his financial crash) Scott was in his day a celebrity. He knew the great men of his time – fellow-writers like Byron and Wordsworth, artists, actors, lawyers and cabinet ministers, Wellington and the Prince Regent. But he was totally unspoiled by success. He was loved by his family, by the people who worked for him and by his Edinburgh and Border neighbours. The great writer never lost the common touch.

This little collection is more concerned with the private man than the author. Most of the quotations in *Sir Walter's Wit and Wisdom* come from letters to friends *(The Letters of Sir Walter Scott*, ed. H.J.C. Grierson, 1936) and from the journal he kept in the last six years of his life. *(The Journal of Sir Walter Scott*, ed. W.E.K.Anderson, Clarendon Press, 1972, and Canongate Press, 1998).

They reveal an endearing as well as a wise and witty character.

THE LIFE OF SIR WALTER SCOTT

1771: born in Edinburgh on 15 August

Spends childhood in Edinburgh and the Borders.

Educated in Kelso, at the High School in Edinburgh and Edinburgh University

Called to the Bar in 1792, appointed Sheriff of Selkirkshire in 1799 and a Principal Clerk of Session in Edinburgh in 1806

Marries Charlotte Carpenter in Carlisle in 1797. Four children: Sophia, Walter, Anne and Charles

Publishes collection of ballads, *The Minstrelsy of the Scottish Border*, 1802

Goes into partnership with James Ballantyne, an old schoolfellow, in printing firm, 1805

Publishes first best-selling narrative poem, *The Lay of the Last Minstrel*, in, 1805, followed over next ten years by *Marmion*, *The Lady of the Lake*, *Rokeby* and *The Lord of the Isles*. Refuses offer of Poet Laureateship in 1813

Rebuilds and enlarges Abbotsford 1812–24

Publishes (anonymously) the first of his novels, *Waverley*, in 1814, followed by *Guy Mannering*, *The Antiquary*, *The Black*

Dwarf, Old Mortality, Rob Roy, The Heart of Mid-Lothian,
The Bride of Lammermoor, A Legend of Montrose, Ivanhoe, The
Monastery, The Abbot, Kenilworth, The Pirate, The Fortunes of
Nigel, Peveril of the Peak, Quentin Durward, St Ronan's Well,
Redgauntlet, The Betrothed, The Talisman, Woodstock, Chronicles
of the Canongate, The Fair Maid of Perth, Anne of Geierstein,
Count Robert of Paris and Castle Dangerous.

Visits the Field of Waterloo and Paris in 1815

Brings to light the royal Regalia of Scotland, 1818; gazetted
Baronet, 1820; attends Coronation of George IV, 1821;
organizes the King's Royal Visit to Edinburgh, 1822

Is financially ruined in January 1826 when his publisher and
printer go bankrupt. Resolves to pay off his own debts and
the debts of both firms by writing for the creditors.

Between 1826 and 1832 publishes six new novels, writes
introductions for first collected edition of his novels, and
publishes a nine-volume *Life of Napoleon, The History of
Scotland, Letters on Demonology and Witchcraft* and *Tales of a
Grandfather*

After severe strokes sails on HMS Barham to Malta and
Naples in search of health, 1831

1832: Returns overland from Rome and dies at
Abbotsford on 21 September.

— ON ABBOTSFORD —

It is a kind of Conundrum Castle to be sure and I have great pleasure in it, for while it pleases a fantastic person in the style and manner of its architecture and decoration it has all the comforts of a commodious habitation.

Journal

— ON ADVERSITY —

In prosperous times I have sometimes felt my fancy and powers of language flag – but adversity is to me at least a tonic and bracer.

Journal

— ON ADVICE —

Good advice is easily followed when it jumps with our own sentiments and inclinations.

Letters

ABBOTSFORD

When Scott bought a little farmhouse in the Scottish Borders in 1812, he renamed it Abbotsford on the grounds that the Abbots of nearby Melrose Abbey, along with everyone else, used to cross the Tweed there in mediaeval times. For the next twelve years every moment that could be spared from writing his novels was devoted to rebuilding and enlarging the house and acquiring land around it. Scott's 'romance in stone' was Scotland's first Scottish baronial mansion. He planted thousands of trees on the estate with his own hand and filled the house with books and curiosities. The mediaeval gloom of stained-glass and panelling was dispelled by gaslight, installed in a house in Scotland for the first time.

Abbotsford, Scott reflected ruefully, was his 'Delilah'. His passion for Abbotsford led him into spending all that he earned from his novels and money he had not yet earned. It was not however the cause of his financial ruin in 1826. His personal debts could have been paid off in a year or two ; his liability for the huge debts incurred by Ballantyne and Constable, his printer and publisher, were the crushing blow.

It was at Abbotsford that Scott died in September 1832, on a warm, still day with the windows open to the sound of the Tweed rippling over its pebbles.

The step of time is noiseless as it passes over an old man.

Journal

Age is easily propitiated by attentions from the young.

Rob Roy

The greatest and wisest are flattered by the deference of youth – so graceful and becoming in itself.

The Abbot

To slacken your hold on life in any agreeable point of connection is the sooner to reduce yourself to the indifference and passive vegetation of old age.

Journal

Nothing in life can be more ludicrous or contemptible than an old man aping the passions of his youth.

Journal

I have often noticed that a kindly placid good humour is the companion of longevity and I suspect frequently the leading cause of it. Quick keen sharp observation with the power of contrast and illustration disturbs this easy current of thought.

Journal

A man of eighty and upwards may be allowed to talk long because in the nature of things he cannot have long to talk.

Journal

In his ninety-second year [*Sir Robert Preston*] has an ample fortune, a sound understanding, not the least decay of eyes ears or taste, is as big as two men and eats like three. Yet ... if his appearance renders old age tolerable it does not make it desirable. But I fear when Death comes we shall be unwilling for all that to part with our bundle of sticks.

Journal

Life is dear even to those who feel it a burden.

The Heart of Mid-Lothian

— ON AMERICANS —

The Americans are so like to the British, the British to the Americans, that they have not much patience with each other for not being in all respects the same with each other.

Letters

I see dissensions between us and the Americans as threatening infinite disadvantage to both Nations and offering no adequate advantage to either.

Letters

AMERICANS

The Waverley Novels were best-sellers in America. Sadly for Scott not a penny came to him in royalties as there was no international copyright law in his day. There was not a great deal of coming and going between Britain and America in Scott's lifetime but Scott's fame attracted several eminent American visitors. Washington Irvine stayed at Abbotsford and wrote about it. Fennimore Cooper, 'the American Scott', met him in London. Audubon, on his first visit to Edinburgh, brought his portfolio of bird pictures to show him. Mark Twain, who never met him, accused Scott of fomenting the Civil War by infecting the South with his notions of bravery and honour. General Lee, it is true, did actually read the Waverley Novels aloud in the evening to his family.

The Americans are a people possessed of very considerable energy quickened and brought into eager action by an honourable love of their country and pride in their institutions but they are as yet rude in their ideas of social intercourse, and totally ignorant speaking generally of all the art of good breeding which consists chiefly in a postponement of one's own petty wishes or comforts to those of others. By rude questions, free and unfeeling observations, an absolute disrespect to other people's feelings and a ready indulgence of their own they make one feverish in their company though perhaps you may be ashamed to confess the reason. But this will wear off and is wearing away.

Letters

— ON ANACHRONISMS —

Poets are at liberty to commit Anachronisms for the sake of effect.

Letters

— ON ANIMOSITY —

Life is too short for the indulgence of animosity.

Letters

— ON ANTIQUARIANISM —

I do not know any thing which relieves the mind so much from the sullens as trifling discussions about antiquarian old-womanries – It is like knitting a stocking, diverting the mind without occupying it.

Journal

— ON JANE AUSTEN —

Reading again and for the third time at least Miss Austen's very finely written novel of *Pride and Prejudice*. That young lady has a talent for describing the involvements and feelings and characters of ordinary life which is to me the most wonderful I ever met with.

Journal

— ON AVARICE —

Avarice seldom sleeps sound.

The Fortunes of Nigel

— ON BABIES —

Mrs Hughes thinks the infant a beauty – Johnie opines that it is not very pretty, and Grandpapa supposes it like other newborn children which are as like as a basket of oranges.

Journal

I care not for children till they care a little for me.

Journal

— ON BAGPIPERS —

Walking within a short interval, and eying each other with looks in which self-importance and defiance might be traced, the bagpipers strutted, puffed, and plied their screaming instruments, each playing his own favourite tune with such a din, that if an Italian musician had lain buried within ten miles of them, he must have risen from the dead to run out of hearing.

The Legend of Montrose

BALLADS

Scott's first literary success was a collection of ballads, *The Minstrelsy of the Scottish Border*.

Ballads were a lifelong passion of Scott's. As a small boy on his grandfather's farm in the Borders (where he spent nearly five of his first seven years in the hope that country air and country food would help cure his lameness) he thrilled to the tales of feuds and Border raids told him by his aunt and his grandmother. As a young man he spent numerous vacations riding to the remotest parts of the Border country in search of the hill-farmers and their wives who could recite or sing ballads handed down orally. Scott collected, among others, 'The Battle of Otterburn' and 'The Wife of Usher's Well', and he wrote songs and ballads of his own like 'Young Lochinvar' and 'Bonnie Dundee'.

— ON BALLADS —

From the earliest period of my existence, ballads and other romantic poems I have read or heard as a favourite and sometimes as an exclusive gratification.

Letters

— ON BEAUTY —

What there is in our partiality to female beauty that commands a species of temperate homage from the aged as well as ecstatic admiration from the young I cannot conceive but it is certain that a very large proportion of some other amiable quality is too little to counterbalance the absolute want of this advantage. I to whom beauty is and shall henceforward be a picture still look upon it with the quiet devotion of an old worshipper.

Journal

Lady Exeter is a beauty after my own heart – a great deal of liveliness in the face – an absence alike of form and of affected ease and really courteous after a genuine and ladylike fashion.

Journal

— ON BEGGING —

I never yield to this importunity, thinking it wrong that what I can spare to meritorious poverty of which I hear and see too much should be diverted by impudent importunity.

Journal

— ON BENEVOLENCE —

The rich much to their honour do not in general require to be so much stimulated to benevolence as to be directed in the most useful way to exert it.

Letters

— ON THE BIBLE —

[*On his deathbed*] He expressed a wish that I should read to him, and when I asked from what book, he said – 'Need you ask? There is but one.'

Lockhart's *Life of Scott*

— ON BORES —

Of all the boring machines ever devised your regular and determined story-teller is the most peremptory and powerful in his operations.

Letters

An efficient bore must always have something respectable about him otherwise no one would permit him to exercise his occupation and bestow his tediousness upon him. He must be for example a very rich man (which perhaps gives the greatest privilege of all) – or he must be a man of rank and condition too important to be treated *sans ceremonie* – or a man of learning (often a dreadful bore) or of talents undoubted and privileged – or of pretensions to wisdom and experience – or a great traveller – In short he must have some tangible privilege to exercise his profession. Without something of this kind one would treat a bore as you do a vagrant mendicant and send him off to the workhouse if he presumed to annoy you.

Letters

— ON BONNIE PRINCE CHARLIE —

I became a valiant Jacobite at the age of ten years old; and, even since reason and reading came to my assistance, I have never quite got rid of the impression which the gallantry of Prince Charles made on my imagination.

Letters

— ON BOSWELL —

Boswell was always labouring at notoriety, and, having failed in attracting it in his own person, he hooked his little bark to them whom he thought most likely to leave harbour, and so shone with reflected light, like the rat that eat the malt that lay in the house that Jack built.

Letters

— ON BOYS —

Boys are uncommonly just in their feelings, and at least equally generous.

Lockhart's *Life of Scott*

— ON BREAKFAST ENTERTAINING —

A neat custom that – and saves wine and wassail.

Journal

— ON BURNS —

Long life to thy fame and peace to thy soul, Rob Burns. When I want to express a sentiment which I feel strongly, I find the phrase in Shakespeare or thee.

Journal

I saw that distinguished poet only once and that many years since. But Burns was so remarkable a man that his features remain impressed on my mind as I had seen him only yesterday.

Letters

I once dined in company with him, and remember well the flash of his dark brown eye. I think his pictures are not like him.

Letters

BURNS

During his visit to Edinburgh in 1786–7 Burns was entertained by Professor Ferguson. Adam Ferguson, his fifteen-year-old son, was Scott's best friend and allowed to invite him to join the party. Burns was impressed by a picture under which there were six lines of verse. 'Who were they by?' he asked. The only person who knew was young Walter Scott.

There is a sad sequel. A few days later Scott saw Burns again in a bookseller's shop. There was no flicker of recognition and the boy did not dare speak to him.

I think it a curious point of Burns' character that he copied over the very same letters or great part of them and sent them to different individuals.

Letters

— ON BYRON —

I felt the prudence of giving way [*as a poet*] before the more forcible and powerful genius of Byron.

Letters

A man of real goodness of heart, and the kindest and best feelings, miserably thrown away by his foolish contempt of public opinion.

Lockhart's *Life of Scott*

What a pity that a man of such exquisite genius will not be contented to be happy on the ordinary terms. I declare my heart bleeds when I think of him, self-banished from the country to which he is an honour.

Letters

— ON CAPRICE —

I have guarded against nothing more in the education of my own family, than against their acquiring habits of self-willed caprice and domination.

Lockhart's Life of Scott

— ON CAUTION —

The Scotch are a cautious people.

Guy Mannering

— ON CATS —

The greatest advance of age which I have yet found is liking a cat an animal I detested and becoming fond of a garden an art which I despised.

Letters

A man of eminence in any line, and perhaps a man of great literary eminence especially, is exposed to a thousand eyes which men, not so celebrated, are safe from – and in consequence, right conduct is much more essential to his happiness than to those who are less watched.

Lockhart's *Life of Scott*

— ON CHAIRMANSHIP —

The meeting was somewhat stormy but I preserved order by listening with patience to each in turn: determined that they should weary out the patience of the meeting before I lost mine. An orator is like a top, let him alone and he must stop one time or another. Flog him and he may go on for ever.

Journal

[*Presiding at public dinners*] I have been rather felicitous not by much superiority of wit and wisdom far less of eloquence. But by two or three simple rules which I put down here for the benefit of posterity … Always hurry the bottle round for five or six rounds without pressing yourself or permitting others to propose. A slight fillip of wine inclines people to be pleased and removes the nervousness which prevents men from speaking – disposes them in short to be amusing and to be amused.. Push on, keep moving, as Punch says – Do not think of saying fine things – nobody cares for them any more than for fine music, which is often too liberally disposed on such occasions. Speak at all ventures and attempt the *mot pour rire*.

You will find people satisfied with wonderfully indifferent jokes if you can but hit the taste of the company, which depends much on its character. Even a very high party primed with all the cold irony and *non est tanti* feelings or no feelings of fashionable folks may be stormed by a jovial rough round and ready *praeses*.

If a drunkard or an ass breaks in with anything out of joint, if you can parry it with a jest, good and well ; if not, do not exert your serious authority unless it is something very bad. The authority even of a chairman ought to be very cautiously exercised. With patience you will have the support of everyone.

When you have drunk a few glasses to play the good fellow and banish modesty if you are unlucky enough to have such a troublesome companion, then beware of the cup too much. Nothing is so ridiculous as a drunken *praeses*.

Lastly always speak short and *Skeoch doch na skial* – cut a tale with a drink.

This is the purpose and intent
— Of gude Schir Walter's testament.

Journal

— ON CHANCE —

O many a shaft at random sent
Finds mark the archer little meant!
And many a word at random spoken
May soothe, or wound, a heart that's broken.

Lord of the Isles

— ON CHESS —

Surely chess-playing is a sad waste of brains.

Lockhart's *Life of Scott*

— ON CHRISTIANITY —

I would if called upon die a martyr for the Christian religion, so completely is (in my poor opinion) its divine origin proved by its beneficial effects on the state of society.

Journal

— ON CLIMBING —

Like an old fool I must needs remember that I was once the best climber in the High School and had even scaled the castle rock by the precarious path called the kittle (i.e. ticklish) nine steps.

Letters

— ON COLERIDGE —

That eccentric but admirable poet, Coleridge.

Letters

I am more and more convinced of the excellence of the English monastic institutions of Cambridge and Oxford. They cannot do all that may be expected but there is at least the exclusion of many temptations to dissipation of minds. Whereas with us, supposing a young man to have any pretensions to keep good society ... he is almost pulled to pieces by speculating mamas and flirting misses. If a man is poor, plain and indifferently connected, he may have excellent opportunities of study at Edinburgh; otherwise he should beware of it.

Letters

When their attentions are to be given to the departments of the cook and the butler all zeal in the nobler paths of education is apt to decay.

Journal

— ON COMMITTEES —

I have no turn for these committees and yet I get always jammed into them. They take up a cruel deal of time in a way very unsatisfactory.

Journal

— ON COMMON PEOPLE —

The common people, the severest critics of the conduct of their betters.

Ivanhoe

How willing the vulgar are to gull themselves when they can find no one else to take the trouble.

Journal

Servants are fond of the woeful: it gives such consequence to the person who communicates.

Journal

— ON COMMON SENSE —

'I'd rather be a kitten, and cry, Mew!' than write the best poetry in the world on condition of laying aside common sense in the ordinary transactions and business of the world.

Letters

Those powers which can make verses are applicable to the more useful and ordinary purposes of life.

Letters

I have always remarked that literary people think themselves obliged to take somewhat of a constrained and affected turn in conversation, seeming to consider themselves as less a part of the company than something which the rest were come to see and wonder at.

Letters

— ON COMPANY —

Few men, leading a quiet life and without any strong or highly varied change of circumstances, have seen more variety of Society than I – few have enjoyed it more or been bored, as it is called, less by the company of tiresome people. I have rarely if ever found anyone out of whom I could not extract amusement or edification.

Journal

I generally affect good spirits in company of my family whether I am enjoying them or not. It is too severe to sadden the harmless mirth of others by suffering your own causeless melancholy to be seen. And this species of exertion is, like virtue, its own reward; for the good spirits which are at first simulated become at length real.

Journal

If the question was eternal company without the power of retiring within yourself or solitary confinement for life I should say 'Turnkey, lock the cell'.

Journal

Solitude has one good thing – it disposes a man to work from which society is sure to divert him.

Letters

The love of solitude increases by indulgence.

Journal

— ON CONVERTS —

I hate a fellow who begins with throwing away his own religion and then affects a prodigious respect for another.

Journal

— ON CONSERVATISM —

The Scotch are not a people who speedily admit innovation, even when it comes in the shape of improvement.

Rob Roy

— ON CONVERSATION —

In general the English understand conversation well. There is that ready deference for the claims of every one who wishes to speak time about.

Journal

The art of quiet and entertaining conversation which is always easy as well as entertaining is I think chiefly known in England. In Scotland we are pedantic and wrangle or run away with the harrows on some topic we chance to be discursive upon. The presence of too many men of distinguished rank and power always freezes the conversation. Each lamp shews brightest when placed by itself; when too close they neutralize each other.

Journal

What a strange scene if the surge of conversation could suddenly ebb like the tide and show us the state of people's real minds ...

> No eyes the rocks discover
> Which lurk beneath the deep.

Life could not be endured were it seen in reality.

Journal

— ON CORPORAL PUNISHMENT —

Many a clever boy is flogged into a dunce and many an original composition corrected into mediocrity.

Journal

I am an enemy to corporal punishment. But there are many boys who will not attend without it. It is an instant and irresistible motive, and I love boys' heads too much to spoil them at the expense of their opposite extremity.

Journal

— ON COUNTRY PLEASURES —

The country is said to be quieter life – not to me I am sure. In the town the business I have to do hardly costs me more thought than just occupies my mind and I have as much of gossip and lady-like chat as consumes the time pleasantly enough. In the country I am thrown entirely on my own resources and there is no medium betwixt happiness and the reverse.

Journal

— ON COURAGE —

That dogged spirit of courage so peculiar to the English
The Betrothed

In literature as in love courage is half the battle.

Journal

It is clear to me that what is least forgiven in a man of any mark or likelihood is want of that article black-guardly called pluck. All the fine qualities of genius cannot make amends for it.

Journal

— ON COURTSHIP —

The truth is, perhaps, the lover's pleasure, like that of the hunter, is in the chase; and that the brightest beauty loses half its merit, as the fairest flower its perfume, when the willing hand can reach it too easily.

Redgauntlet

— ON CRITICISM —

I make it a rule never to read the attacks made upon me.

Letters

A third rogue writes to tell me that he approves of the first three volumes of the *Heart of Mid-Lothian* but totally condemns the fourth ... However an author should be reasonably well pleased when three fourths of his works are acceptable to the reader.

Journal

— ON DEATH —

And come he slow, or come he fast,
It is but Death who comes at last.

Marmion

When musing on companions gone
We doubly feel ourselves alone.

Marmion

[*On his deathbed, to Lockhart*:] Be a good man – be virtuous – be religious – be a good man. Nothing else will
give you any comfort when you come to lie here.

Lockhart's *Life of Scott*

— ON DEBT —

The mere scarcity of money (so that actual wants are
provided) is not poverty. It is the bitter draught to owe
money which we cannot pay.

Journal

DEBT

Scott knew about debt from bitter experience. At the height of his fame the recession of 1826 bankrupted his printer and his publisher. There being no limited liability in those days, Scott, who was a partner in his printer's enterprise, found himself liable for the debts of both firms, £127,000 in all. Instead of declaring himself bankrupt and re-establishing his fortune with his pen, he decided that the honourable course was to shoulder the burden and repay the money by writing for his creditors. 'No! This right hand shall work it all off', he vowed. It was an extraordinarily noble resolution. But to have done otherwise, he said, 'I would in a Court of Honour deserve to lose my spurs.'

The debt was finally extinguished, partly by the sale of the books he published between 1826 and 1832 and partly by the sale of the copyrights of his novels to his publisher after his death.

— ON DECEIT —

O what a tangled web we weave,
When first we practise to deceive!

Marmion

— ON DEMOCRACY —

Royal magnificence can be only displayed by despotic power. In England, were the most splendid street or public building to be erected the matter must be discussed in parliament or perhaps some sturdy cobbler holds out and refuses to part with his stall and the whole plan is disconcerted. Long may such impediments exist.

Journal

— ON DENTISTS —

He that has rid a man of the tooth-ache is well entitled to command a part of his time.

Journal

— ON DETERMINATION —

[*After the financial crash.*] But I will involve no friend either rich or poor – My own right hand shall do it.

Journal

The great art of life, so far as I have been able to observe, consists in fortitude and perseverance.

Letters

Men of genius are not only equally fit but much fitter for the business of the world than dunces, providing always they will give their talents fair play by curbing them with application.

Letters

There is usually an obstinacy in weakness.

Journal

— ON DOING GOOD —

If we do not run some hazard in our attempts to do good where is the merit of them?

Journal

— ON DRAMA —

I am very fond of the Stage which is the only public amusement that I ever indulge in.

Letters

After all as times go the applause of a London audience is so little to be desired that it has always appeared to me that writing for the stage is a most desperate business.

Letters

Making any serious theatrical attempt is as much out of my mind as flying in a balloon.

Letters

To write for low, ill-informed, and conceited actors, whom you must please, for your success is necessarily at their mercy, I cannot away with. Besides, if this objection were out of the way, I do not think the character of the audience in London is such that one could have the least pleasure in pleasing them.

Letters

— ON DUTY —

No good man can ever be happy when he is unfit for the career of simple and commonplace duty, and I need not add how many melancholy instances there are of extravagance and profligacy being resorted to, under the pretence of contempt for the common rules of life.

Letters

I shall do my duty however. Do what is right come what will.

Journal

Such dusky grandeur clothed the height,
Where the huge Castle holds its state,
And all the steep slope down,
Whose ridgy back heaves to the sky,
Piled deep and massy, close and high,
Mine own romantic town.

Marmion

[*An Edinburgh father's judgement on his son's scapegrace friend*] He has little solidity, Alan, little solidity.

Redgauntlet

— ON EDUCATION —

Habits of firm and assiduous application, of gaining the art of controlling, directing and concentrating the powers of his mind for earnest investigation is an art far more essential than even that intimate acquaintance with classical learning, which is the primary object of study.

Waverley

It is an old proverb, used by Chaucer and quoted by Elizabeth, that 'the greatest clerks are not the wisest men'; and it is as true as if the poet had not rhymed, or the queen reasoned on it.

The Monastery

My education was of a very desultory nature not from want of the kindest paternal care but, partly from bad health in early youth, partly from the interruptions seclusions and indulgences, I was too much permitted to study what I liked, and when I liked, which was very little and very seldom. To mend the matter I stuffed my brains with all such reading as was never read and in the department of my memory where should be a Roman Patera Lo! there is a witches' cauldron. I am more apt to pray to Thor or Woden than Jupiter, think of the fairies oftener than the Dryads and of Bannockburn and Flodden more than Marathon and Pharsalia.

Letters

To give education to dull mediocrity is a flinging of the children's bread to dogs – it is sharpening a hatchet on a razor-strop, which renders a strop useless and does no good to the hatchet.

Journal

All men who have turned out worth anything have had the chief hand in their own education.

Letters

— ON ENGLAND —

England was merry England, when
Old Christmas brought his sport again.
'Twas Christmas broached the mightiest ale;
'Twas Christmas told the merriest tale;
A Christmas gambol oft could cheer
The poor man's heart through half the year.

Marmion

— ON ENGLISH BOYS —

Well mannered and sensible are the Southern boys.
I suppose the sun brings them forwards.

Journal

ENGLAND

Not every Scot loves the English countryside and the English character as much as Scott did. He was Scottish to the core but no narrow nationalist.

With the French Revolution and Napoleon closing the continent for nearly a quarter of a century to English travellers, many came instead to Edinburgh, the 'Athens of the North'. So from his youth Scott had several English friends. His narrative poems, especially *The Lay of the Last Minstrel*, *Marmion* and *The Lady of the Lake*, took the English reading public by storm, and on each of his five visits to England he found that he was a celebrity. He was invited to the Coronation of George IV, and on a later visit to London his *Journal* records social engagements with Canning, Peel, Wordsworth, Lawrence and dozens of the other great men of the time.

English boys have this advantage that they are well bred and can converse when ours are regular-built cubs – I am not sure if it is an advantage in the long run. It is a temptation to premature display.

Journal

— ON ENGLISH CHURCHES —

One of those old-fashioned Gothic parish churches which are frequent in England, the most cleanly, decent, and reverential places of worship that are, perhaps, anywhere to be found in the Christian world.

The Heart of Mid-Lothian

— ON ENGLISHMEN —

As far as I have observed no two nations in Europe resemble each other less that the English and Scotch – I mean the middle classes, for those of the highest ranks by travel and company soon rub off all marks of Nationality. The Englishman is very apt to partake of the feelings of those around him and nowhere is a popular impulse so universally acknowledged. Now my Countrymen are sly restive and contradictory in their dispositions and I sincerely believe that utter starvation will hardly bring twelve of them to unite in one verdict unless their national pride is concerned in the question in which cause an hundred will have but one voice.

Letters

My countrymen, taken in their general capacity, are not people to have recourse to in adverse circumstances. John Bull is a better beast in misfortune.

Letters

Every Englishman has a tolerably accurate sense of law and justice.

The Two Drovers

The Englishman's characteristic of More Money than wit.

Journal

— ON ENVY —

I have sometimes envied rich citizens but it was a mean and erroneous feeling. Better be a poor gentleman after all.

Journal

— ON ETON —

The talents, good sense and knowledge of the world, picked up at one of the great English schools (and it is one of their most important results) will prevent him from being deceived.

Journal

— ON EVIL —

Where the heart is prepared for evil, opportunity is seldom long wanting.

The Heart of Mid-Lothian

— ON EXERTION —

Exertion, like virtue, is its own reward.

Waverley

— ON FAME —

Fame depends on literature not on architecture.

Journal

If there be any great advantage in literary fame I have had it and I certainly do not care at losing it. They cannot say but what I *had* the *crown*.

Journal

— ON FAREWELLS —

I hate red eyes and blowing of noses.

Journal

— ON FATE —

Twist ye, twine ye! even so
Mingle shades of joy and woe,
Hope and fear, and peace and strife,
In the thread of human life.

Guy Mannering

— ON FAVOURS —

Enough ill nature to keep your good nature from being abused is no bad ingredient in their disposition who have favours to bestow.

Journal

— ON FATHERS —

Breakfasted with Charles in his Chambers where he had everything very neat – how pleasant it is for a father to sit at his child's board! It is like the aged man reclining under the shadow of the oak which he has planted,

Journal

— ON FAVOURITES —

Although a favourite, as the poet assures us, has no friend, he seldom fails to have both followers and flatterers.

The Fortunes of Nigel

— ON FOOLS —

A wise man will receive information and fresh views of life even in the Society of Fools.

Journal

Talking of Abbotsford it begins to be haunted by too much company of every kind. But especially foreigners. I do not like them. I hate fine waistcoats and breast pins upon dirty shirts.

Journal

I make it a rule seldom to read and never to answer foreign letters from literary folk. It leads to nothing but the battledore and shuttlecock intercourse of compliments as light as cork and feathers.

Journal

Those who wish to see me should be able to speak my language.

Journal

— ON FRANCE —

Ere I leave la belle France however it is fit I should express my gratitude for the unwontedly kind reception which I met with at all hands. I would be an unworthy piece of affectation did I not allow that I have been pleased – highly pleased – to find a species of literature intended only for my own country had met such an extensive and favourable reception in a foreign land where there was so much *a priori* to oppose its progress.

Journal

— ON FRENCH —

The French language is certainly the most unfit for Poetry that ever was uttered. I do not believe there are twenty words in the language that can be properly termed poetical, that is that are not equally used in Poetry or Prose, and this alone gives poverty and meanness to their verses.

Letters

— ON FRIENDSHIP —

The chain of friendship however bright does not stand the attrition of constant close contact.

Journal

— ON FUNERALS —

I hate funerals – always did. There is such a mixture of mummery with real grief – the actual mourner perhaps heart broken and all the rest making solemn faces and whispering observations on the weather and public news and here and there a greedy fellow enjoying the cake and wine … This is a most unfilial tendency of mine for my father absolutely loved a funeral and as he

was a man of a fine presence and looked the mourner
well he was asked to every interment of distinction. He
seemed to preserve the list of a whole bead roll of cous-
ins merely for the pleasure of being at their funerals,
which he was often asked to superintend and I suspect
had sometimes to pay for.

Journal

— ON GARDENS —

The greatest advance of age which I have yet found is liking a cat an animal I detested and becoming fond of a garden an art which I despised.

Letters

— ON GEORGE III —

The excellent private character of the Old King gave him great advantages as the Head of a free government. I fear the [New King] will long experience the inconveniences of not having attended to his own.

Letters

Old farmer George's manly simplicity, modesty of expense and domestic virtue saved this country at its most perilous crisis.

Letters

GEORGE IV

One of the redeeming features of the portly, dissolute and extravagant Prince Regent is that he was an ardent admirer of Scott's poems and novels. He invited Scott to visit him in London and Windsor; bestowed the first Baronetcy of his reign on him and made the first modern Royal Visit to Scotland, probably at Scott's suggestion.

Well-schooled by what he had read in *The Lady of the Lake*, *Waverley* and *Rob Roy*, he arrived in Edinburgh equipped with two complete Highland Dress outfits and one hundred and nine yards of Royal Stuart tartan. The cartoonists had a field day. So did Scott who organized the whole fortnight of processions, dinners, drawing-rooms and levees, as well as a visit to the theatre to see *Rob Roy*. (The King enjoyed the play. 'It was', he said, 'neither too long nor too short.')

— ON GEORGE IV —

He converses with so much ease and elegance that you lose thoughts of the prince in admiring the well-bred and accomplished gentleman. He is in many respects the model of a British monarch.

Journal

— ON GERMANS —

There are no braver men than the Germans.

The Talisman

— ON GHOSTS —

Ghosts are only seen where they are believed.

Letters

— ON GOD —

I believe in God who can change evil into good and I am confident that what befalls us is always ultimately for the best.

Journal

God help – but rather God bless – man must help himself.

Journal

— ON GOETHE —

Goethe, an author born to arouse the slumbering fame of his country.

Anne of Geierstein

Goethe is different and a wonderful fellow, the Ariosto at once, and almost the Voltaire of Germany.

Journal

— ON GOOD LISTENERS —

My new daughter-in-law seems quite alert at everything but talking much. A good listener is no bad thing however, and she always laughs in the right place.

Letters

— ON GRAMMAR —

I write grammar as I speak, to make my meaning known, and a solecism in point of composition like a Scotch word in speaking is indifferent to me.

Journal

The study of grammar from its very asperities is calculated to teach youth that patient labour which is necessary to the useful exertion of the understanding upon every other branch of knowledge.

Letters

— ON GRATITUDE —

I never have yet found that ill-will dies in debt or what is called gratitude distresses herself by frequent payments.

Journal

The time devoted to hospitality, especially to those whom I can reckon upon as sincere good friends, I never grudge but I like to —

Welcome the coming speed the parting guest.

Journal

HAIL TO THE CHIEF

How did four words written by Scott become associated with the President of the United States?

When *The Lady of the Lake* was turned into a melodrama in London and New York, James Sanderson set to music the boating-song of the Highland chieftain in the poem and published it as sheet music in Philadelphia in 1812. Three years later it was played as a welcome to President Washington. The tune soon became the traditional anthem of successive Presidents of the United States. Although other verses have been written to fit the tune they are not usually performed. So the only words always associated with it are still Scott's 'Hail to the Chief'.

Hail to the Chief, who in triumph advances.

The Lady of the Lake

— ON HANDWRITING —

This hand of mine gets to be like a kitten's scratch and will require much deciphering, or what may be as well for the writer, cannot be deciphered at all. I am sure I cannot read it myself.

Journal

— ON HEAVEN —

They have a poor idea of the Deity and the rewards that are destined for the Just made perfect who can only adopt the literal sense of an eternal concert – a never-ending Birthday Ode. I rather suppose there should be understood some commission from the Highest, some duty to discharge with the applause of a satisfied conscience. There would be, we must suppose, in these employments difficulties to be overcome and exertions to be made.

Journal

— ON HIGHLANDERS —

In giving an account of a Highlander, his pedigree is first to be considered.

Rob Roy

There are few nations, by the way, who can boast of so much natural politeness as the Highlanders.

Waverley

— ON HONOURS —

[*On being gazetted Baronet*:] Remember I anticipate the jest 'I like not such grinning honour as Sir Walter hath'.

Letters

— ON HUNTING —

Riding haill days after a bit beast than winna weigh sax punds when they hae catched it.

Andrew Fairservice in *Rob Roy*

In every point of view field-sports are preferable to the in-door amusement of a Billiards table, which is too often the lounging place for idle young officers where there is nothing to be got but a habit of throwing away time and an acquaintance with the very worst society.

Letters

Ladies whose husbands love foxhunting are in a poor way. They manage the matter otherwise in France where Ladies are the Lords of the Ascendant.

Journal

— ON HYMNS —

I think those hymns which do not immediately recall the warm and exalted language of the Bible are apt to be, however elegant, rather cold and flat for the purposes of devotion.

Letters

I

— ON IDLENESS —

Our time is like our money. When we change a guinea the shillings escape as things of small account. When we break a day by idleness in the morning the rest of the hours lose their importance in our eye.

Journal

If you once turn on your side after the hour at which you ought to rise, it is all over. Bolt up at once.

Journal

[*Scott's practice*] Never to be doing nothing.

Letters

— ON INDUSTRIALIZATION —

Nature intended that population should be diffused over the soil in proportion to its extent. We have accumulated in huge cities and smothering manufacturies the number which should be spread over the face of a country and what wonder that they should be corrupted?

Journal

— ON INTERRUPTIONS —

There is a great pleasure in sitting down to write with the consciousness that nothing will occur during the day to break the spell.

Journal

After all these interruptions are not such bad things – they make a man keen of the work which he is with-held from – you stick to it for contradiction's sake.

Journal

— ON THE IRISH —

I am much honoured by the good opinion of the Irish nation whose praise must be always most valuable to a poet because they are not only a people of infinite genius but of a warmth of heart and feeling not per-haps generally appreciated either by your countrymen or mine.

Letters

The inhabitants, from the peer to the peasant, are cer-tainly the kindest people in the world.

Letters

IRELAND

The summer before the collapse of his finances, Scott visited Ireland to see his son Walter who had been posted there with his regiment. He received a rapturous welcome. He was given an honorary degree, church bells rang for him and crowds cheered him in the street. He already had several Irish friends, including the novelist Maria Edgeworth and Thomas Moore the poet, but the visit made him delight more than ever in Irish liveliness and humour.

I do not think even our Scottish hospitality can match that of Ireland.

Letters

They are certainly a very odd people and but for that ugly humour of murdering which is in full decline they would be the most amusing and easy to live with in the world.

Letters

While a Scotchman is thinking about the term day, or if easy on that subject about Hell in the next world, while an Englishman is making a little hell of his own in the present because his muffin is not well roasted,

Pat's mind is always turned to fun and ridicule. They are terribly excitable to be sure and will murther you on slight suspicion and find out next day that it was all a mistake and that it was not yourself they meant to kill at all at all.

Journal

The protestants of the old school, or determined Orangemen, are a very fine race but dangerous for the quiet of a country.

Letters

I do not believe either party care a bit for what is called emancipation only that the Catholics desire it because the protestants are not willing they should have it and the protestants desire to withhold it because the want of it mortifies the Catholics.

Letters

— ON ITALIANS —

Are not you sensible of the difference between language and language when turning from even the best French Poets to the richness of the Italians? The difference in their music or in their painting is scarce more remarkable – it is positive repose and enjoyment – there is something hard and meagre and cold and affected in the French diction.

Letters

It is mortifying that Dante seemed to think nobody worth being sent to hell but his own Italians, whereas other people had every bit as great rogues in their families, whose misdeeds were suffered to pass with impunity.

Lockhart's Life of Scott

— ON JACOBITES —

Any success I may have had in hitting off the Stuarts is, I am afraid, owing to a little old Jacobite leaven which I sucked in with the numerous traditionary tales that amused my infancy.

Letters

A tincture of Jacobitism, though rather an Instinct than a principle adopted from reason, forms a frequent feature in the character of the animal called a thorough bred Scotsman.

Letters

I was always a willing listener to tales of broil and battle and hubbub of every kind and now I look back on it I think what a godsend I must have been while a boy to the old Trojans of 1745, nay 1715, who used to frequent my father's house and who knew as little as I did for what market I was laying up the raw materials of their oft told tales.

Letters

— ON JEDBURGH JUSTICE —

The criminals came in so fast that they were fain to execute them first and afterwards try them at leisure.

Letters

— ON JEWS —

[The Jew] had upon his side the unyielding obstinacy of his nation, and that unbending resolution, with which Israelites have been frequently known to submit to the uttermost evils which power and violence can inflict upon them, rather than gratify their oppressors by granting their demands.

Ivanhoe

— ON DR JOHNSON —

Johnson's rudeness possibly arose from his retaining till late in life the habits of a pedagogue, who is a man among boys and a boy among men, and having the bad taste to think it more striking to leap over the little differences and courtesies which form the turnpike gates in society, and which fly open on payment of a trifling tribute.

Letters

The best of luxuries, the luxury of knowledge.

Guy Mannering

— ON LANDSEER —

Landseer's dogs were the most magnificent things I ever saw, leaping and bounding and grinning on the canvas.

Journal

— ON LAUGHTER —

Real laughter is a thing as rare as real tears.

Journal

Good humour can spread a certain inexpressible charm over the plainest human countenance.

The Black Dwarf

— ON LAW —

Mrs Bertram: That sounds like nonsense, my dear.
Mr Bertram: May be so, my dear; but it may be very good law for all that.

Guy Mannering

LAWYERS

Scott, who was the son of an Edinburgh solicitor, a Writer to the Signet, studied classics, philosophy and law at Edinburgh University and was called to the Bar as an advocate. Because of two desirable legal appointments he did not however practice long as a barrister.

At the age of twenty-eight he was appointed Sheriff of Selkirkshire, charged with enquiring into cases of assault or riotous behaviour, and presiding in his local court and at parliamentary elections. Some years later he became a Principal Clerk of Session in Scotland's main law courts in Edinburgh. The duties were to ensure that the proper legal procedures were followed in each case and to record the judgement in the correct form. These appointments gave Scott a decent income, and an obligation to spend half the year in Edinburgh and half in the Borders. As the Court of Session sat for only three hours a day and twenty-two weeks in the year and as he was allowed to appoint a deputy in Selkirk, he also had time to write. Scott denied that he ever wrote novels in court but admitted to writing letters if a case was lengthy and tedious.

The trials of Fergus McIvor in *Waverley* and of Jeanie Deans in *The Heart of Mid-Lothian* and the never-ending case of Puir Peter Peebles in *Redgauntlet* are clearly the work of a writer who was also a lawyer.

A lawyer without history or literature is a mechanic, a mere working mason; if he possesses some knowledge of these, he may venture to call himself an architect.

Guy Mannering

One can easily, I am assured, get into a lawsuit – it is only the getting out which is sometimes found troublesome.

Redgauntlet

There is something sickening in seeing poor devils drawn into great expense about trifles by interested attorneys. But too cheap access to litigation has its evils on the other hand, for the proneness of the lower class to gratify spite and revenge in this way would be a dreadful evil were they able to endure the expense.

Journal

Most attorneys have been suspected, more or less justly, of making their own fortunes at the expense of their clients.

Lockhart's *Life of Scott*

They are funny people the Americans: I saw a paper in which they said my father was a tailor. If he had been an honest tailor, I should not have been ashamed of the circumstance; but he was what may be thought as great a phenomenon, for he was an honest lawyer, a cadet of a good family, whose predecessors only dealt in pinking and slashing doublets, not in making them.

Letters

[Legal business] keeps one however in the career and stream of actual life, which is a great advantage to a literary man.

Journal

A barrister of extended practice if he has any talents at all is the best companion in the world.

Journal

The wigs against the wits for a guinea in point of conversation.

Journal

I suppose I am partial but I think the lawyers beat the bishops and the bishops beat the wits.

Journal

— ON LEARNING —

'Learning is better than house or land.'

quoted in *Letters*

— ON LEISURE —

To enjoy leisure, it is absolutely necessary it should be preceded by occupation.

The Monastery

— ON LETTERS —

Writing to one's friends is the next thing to seeing them.

Letters

I detest letter writing and envy the Old Hermit of Prague who never saw pen or ink.

Journal

— ON LIFE —

Sound, sound the clarion, fill the fife!
To all the sensual world proclaim:
One crowded hour of glorious life
Is worth an age without a name.

Old Mortality

— ON LITERARY PEOPLE —

When I first saw that a literary profession was to be my fate I endeavoured by all efforts of stoicism to divest myself of that irritable degree of sensibility – or to speak plainly of Vanity – which makes the poetical race miserable and ridiculous.

Journal

[Thomas Moore and I] have both seen the world too widely and too well not to contemn in our souls the imaginary consequence of literary people who walk with their noses in the air.

Journal

I do not incline to make what is called literary acquaintances.

Journal

I have always felt the value of having access to persons of talent and genius to be the best part of a literary man's prerogative.

Letters

— ON LONDON —

London licks the butter off our bread by opening a better market for ambition. Were it not for the difference of the religion and laws poor Scotland could hardly keep a man that is worth having.

Journal

That immense hash of a city.

Journal

A yellow fog which is the curse of London. I would hardly take my share of it for a share of its wealth and its curiosity, a vile double distilled fog of the most intolerable kind.

Journal

But who cares for the whipped cream of London Society?

Journal

To be acquainted with persons of mere *ton* is a nuisance and a scrape – to be known to persons of real fashion and fortune is in London a great advantage.

Journal

I would like to be there were it but to see how the cat jumps. One knows nothing of the world if you are absent from it so long as I have been.

Journal

A Londoner with all the acuteness, address, and audacity which belong peculiarly to the youth of a metropolis.

The Fortunes of Nigel

— ON LOOKING FOR THINGS —

I was *l'homme qui cherche* this morning. There is a conspiracy by which those papers you seek creep out of the way and those you are not wanting perk themselves in your face again and again until at last you throw them into some corner in a passion and then they are the objects of research in their turn.

Journal

— ON LOVE —

True love's the gift which God has given
To man alone beneath the heaven.

Lay of the Last Minstrel

— ON LUCK —

I love marks of good luck even in trifles.

Journal

— ON MADNESS —

Women it is said go mad much seldomer than men.

Journal

— ON MARRIAGE —

Scarce one person out of twenty marries his first love, and scarce one out of the twenty of the remainder has cause to rejoice in having done so.

Letters

The happiest marriages I have seen have been those which began under circumstances which required economy.

Letters

— ON MELROSE —

If thou wouldst view fair Melrose aright,
Go visit it by the pale moonlight;
For the gay beams of lightsome day
Gild, but to flout, the ruins grey.

Lay of the Last Minstrel

— ON MEN —

I like to see men think and bear themselves like men.

Journal

Strong men are usually good-humoured and active men often display the same elasticity of mind as of body.

Journal

The subject of foreign news and the political and military situation of the country are themes upon which every man thinks himself qualified to give an opinion.

The Antiquary

— ON METHODISTS —

They have their faults and are peculiarly liable to those of hypocrisy and spiritual ambition and priest-craft. On the other hand they do infinite good, carrying religion into classes in Society where it would scarce be found to penetrate did it rely merely upon proof of its doctrines upon calm reason and upon rational argument. To these the Methodists add a powerful appeal to the feelings and passions and though I believe this is often exaggerated into absolute enthusiasm yet I consider upon the whole they do much to keep alive a sense of religion and the practice of morality necessarily connected with it.

Journal

— ON MISANTHROPY —

Misanthropy ... I always consider as a kind of blasphemy of a shocking description. If God bears with the very worst of us we may surely endure each other. If thrown into society I always have and always will endeavour to bring pleasure with me, at least to shew willingness to please. But for all this 'I had rather live alone'.

Journal

— ON MONEY —

I have arrived at a flocci-pauci-nihili-pili-fication of money and I thank Shenstone for inventing that long word.

Journal

Capital and talent will do excellent things together; but depend on it, talent without capital will no more carry on an extensive and progressive undertaking than a racehorse will draw a Newcastle wagon.

Letters

— ON MUSIC —

Where there is a natural turn this way it is a great pity not to cultivate it. There is such a thing as singing the evil spirit out of others or oneself. In fact I think music (not cultivated to excess or made the introduction to too much idleness or, in men, conviviality) has a moral effect on the spirits and temper.

Letters

I do not know and cannot utter a note of music and complicated harmonies seem to me a babble of confused though pleasing sounds. Yet songs and simple melodies especially if connected with words and ideas have as much effect on me as on most people.

Journal

My ear appears to me as dull as my voice is incapable of musical expression and yet I feel the utmost pleasure in any such music as I can comprehend, learned pieces always excepted.

Journal

I have an indifferent good ear for a jig, but your solos and sonatas give me the spleen.

(adapted from Congreve's *Love for Love) Letters*

I have a wretched ear myself, yet have great pleasure in some passages. This circumstance is the more provoking, as I believe no man in Britain had more songs of all kinds by heart than I could have mustered.

Letters

— ON MUSES —

I don't wonder, that, in dismissing all the other deities of Paganism, the Muse should have been retained by common consent; for, in sober reality, writing good verses seems to depend upon something separate from the volition of the author.

Letters

— ON NAPLES —

Much struck with the beauty of the Bay of Naples.
It is insisted that my arrival has been a signal for the
greatest eruption from Vesuvius which that mountain
has favoured us with for many a day. I can only say as
the Frenchman said of the comet supposed to foretell
his own death, '*Ah, Messieurs, la Comète me fait trop
d'honneur.*'

Journal

— ON NAPOLEON —

He might have been a great man and was only a great
soldier – he might have been the benefactor of the
human race and he was the cause of more blood being
spilled than had flowed for an hundred years before.
He lowered the standard of virtue and public feeling
among the French and soiled their soldierly character
by associating it with perfidy and dishonour.

Letters

NAPOLEON

Napoleon cast a long shadow over the life of Britain for some twenty years. The threat of invasion was as real as Hitler's in 1940 and Napoleon's army seemed as invincible.

The Edinburgh Volunteer Dragoons were among the many bodies enlisted to defend the country, and Scott (who was prevented only by his childhood lameness from becoming a soldier) trained with them on Portobello sands and acted as their quartermaster. Shortly after Wellington's victory in 1815 Scott visited the field of Waterloo. He was fascinated by Buonaparte and published a nine-volume *Life of Napoleon* in 1829.

Napoleon's pen-case and a lock of his hair are on display at Abbotsford.

There will be no permanent peace in Europe till Buonaparte sleeps with the tyrants of old.

Letters

Although too much of a soldier among sovereigns, no-one could claim with better right to be a sovereign among soldiers.

Life of Napoleon

But if Boney and his invincibles did not come to share the fate of

> 'Alexander, king of Macedon,
> — Who conquered all the world but
> Scotland alone'

why, it was not my fault; we dreamed of him, looked for him, and, by our Lady, hoped for him.

Letters

— ON NECESSITY —

Necessity – thou best of peacemakers, as well as surest prompter of invention.

Peveril of the Peak

No whetter of genius is necessity though said to be the mother of invention.

Journal

— ON OPERA —

[*A performance of Ivanhoe in Paris.*] It was an opera and of course the story greatly mangled and the dialogue in a great part nonsense.

Journal

— ON ORATORY —

Many men care less to gain their point than they do to play the orator and be listened to for a certain time.

Journal

An orator is like a top: let him alone and he must stop one time or another. Flog him and he may go on for ever.

Journal

OPERA

For all his professed dislike of opera Scott inspired more operas – some ninety in all – than any writer other than Shakespeare. Of those that are still occasionally performed the best-known are Sullivan's *Ivanhoe*, Bizet's *Jolie Fille de Perth* and Donizetti's *Lucia di Lammermoor*.

— ON ORDERLINESS —

I have had all my life a longing to do some thing else when I am called to particular labour – a vile contradictory humour which I cannot get rid of.

Journal

Though I always wonder why it should be so I feel a dislike to order and to task work of all kinds … what I mean is a detestation of precise order in petty matters – in reading or answering letters, in keeping my papers arranged and in order and so on.

Journal

— ON ORDINATION —

It is *entre nous* a sneaking line unless the adoption of it is dictated by a strong feeling of principle.

Letters

The view of Oxford from the Maudlin Bridge which I
used to think one of the most beautiful in the world.

Journal

— ON PAINTING —

A painting should to be excellent have something to say to the mind of a man like myself, well educated and susceptible to those feelings of which anything recalling natural emotion is likely to inspire. But how seldom do I see anything that moves me much.

Journal

— ON PARIS —

Paris I am not anxious to see again but I trust you will see it once. There is more of good and bad in it than anywhere else in the world. I do not mean moral good of which there is rather a paucity but worldly grandeur and display.

Letters

Of all capitals, that of France affords most numerous objects of curiosity, accessible in the easiest manner, and it may be therefore safely pronounced one of the most entertaining places of residence which can be chosen by an idle man.

Paul's Letters to his Kinsfolk

— ON PATRIOTISM —

Breathes there the man, with soul so dead,
Who never to himself hath said,
This is my own, my native land!
Whose heart hath ne'er within him burned
As home his footsteps he hath turned
From wandering on a foreign strand!
If such there breathe, go, mark him well;
For him no Minstrel raptures swell;
High though his titles, proud his name,
Boundless his wealth as wish can claim;
Despite those titles, power, and pelf,
The wretch concentred all in self,
Living, shall forfeit fair renown,
And, doubly dying, shall go down
To the vile dust, from whence he sprung,
Unwept, unhonoured, and unsung.

The Lay of the Last Minstrel

— ON PEACE —

I used to be fond of war when I was a younger man, and longed heartily to be a soldier; but now I think there is no prayer in the service with which I could close more earnestly, than 'Send peace in our time, good Lord'.

Letters

— ON PERTHSHIRE —

Perthshire forms the fairest portion of the northern kingdom.

The Fair Maid of Perth

— ON PHILOSOPHY —

Of what use is philosophy, and I have always pretended to a little of a practical character, if it cannot teach us to do or suffer?

Journal

— ON PLOTS —

I am but too conscious of having considered the plot only as what Bayes calls the means of bringing in fine things.

Journal

Now this may seem strange but it is quite true, and it is no less so that I have generally written to the middle of one of these novels without having the least idea how it was to end, in short in the *Der donde diere* or hab nab at a venture style of compositions.

Journal

I never yet began a poem upon a preconcerted story, and have often been well-advanced in composition before I had any idea how I was to end the work.

Letters

— ON POETRY —

Teach your children poetry; it opens the mind, lends grace to wisdom and makes the heroic virtues hereditary.

Letters

Did any of my sons show poetical talent of which (to my great satisfaction) there are no appearances, the first thing I should do would be to inculcate upon him the duty of cultivating some honourable profession and qualifying himself to play a more respectable part in Society than the mere poet.

Letters

One poet should always speak for another.

Journal

The country is by all good citizens despaired of once every twenty years by all men claiming a title to the least knowledge on the subject and has always hitherto *righted* of her own accord without much assistance from the crew and sometimes when their strength was employed in a direction that would have swamped her.

Letters

The adaptation of religious motives to earthly policy is apt – among the infinite delusions of the human heart – to be a snare.

Journal

One individual always manages his own concerns better than those of the country can be managed.

Letters

Your deepest pools, like your deepest politicians and philosophers, often turn out more shallow than expected.

Journal

— ON THE POOR —

I have heard higher sentiments from the lips of poor uneducated men and women, when exerting the spirit of severe yet gentle heroism under difficulties and afflictions, or speaking their simple thoughts as to circumstances in the lot of friends and neighbours, than I ever yet met with out of the pages of the Bible.

Lockhart's Life of Scott

— ON POPULARITY —

But no one shall find me rowing against the stream. I care not who knows it – I write for the general amusement.

The Fortunes of Nigel

— ON PRAISE —

I think I make no habit of feeding on praise, and despise those whom I see greedy for it as I should an underbred fellow who after eating a cherry-tart proceeded to lick the plate. But when one is flagging, a little praise (if it can be had genuine and unadulterated by flattery which is as difficult to come by as the genuine Mountain dew) is a cordial after all.

Journal

No man that ever wrote a line despised the pap of praise so heartily as I do.

Journal

I have endeavoured with some success never to trouble myself about fashionable applause or censure or parodies or commendatory verses or being praised in one review or blamed in another.

Letters

[*French flattery*] One can swallow a great deal of whipped cream to be sure and it does not hurt an old stomach.

[*One day later*] I wish for a little of the old Scotch causticity. I am something like the bee that sips treacle.

Journal

— ON PRESERVATION —

Am clear in my own mind a ruin should be protected but never repaired.

Journal

— ON THE PRESS —

The Newspaper told about fifty lies about this matter as usual but one would have little to do who should mind them.

Letters

Nothing but a thorough-going Blackguard ought to attempt the daily press.

Journal

— ON PRINTING —

I love to have the press thumping, clattering and banging in my rear – it creates the necessity which almost always makes me work best.

Journal

— ON PROFESSIONS —

I myself detested the profession of the bar to which I was bred up.

Letters

My supposed poetical turn ruined me in my profession. The commencement of every profession is necessarily dull and disagreeable to youths of lively genius.

Letters

Bookselling is the most ticklish and unsafe and hazardous of all professions scarcely with the exception of horse-jockeyship.

Letters

I have never remarked anyone, be he soldier or divine or lawyer, that was exclusively attached to the narrow habits of his own profession, but what such person became a great twaddle in good society, besides, what is of much more importance, becoming narrow-minded and ignorant of all general information.

Letters

— ON PROMISES —

Promises made to young folk should always be solemnly observed.

Letters

— ON PSALMS —

Let them write hymns and paraphrases if they will but let us have still

'All people on the earth that dwell.'

Journal

— ON PUBLIC DINNERS —

Dined at a public dinner ... An odd way of testifying respect to publick characters by eating drinking and roaring.

Journal

— ON PUBLISHERS —

A Bookseller publishes twenty Books in hopes of hitting upon one good speculation as a person buys a parcel of shares in a lottery in hopes of gaining a prize.

Journal

PUBLISHERS

Archibald Constable, 'the Napoleon of booksellers', made a fortune for Scott and then bankrupted him. He was a larger-than-life character who thought big and hated to admit failure. After the firm collapsed in 1826 piles of unsold books, whose failure to sell he had concealed, were discovered. Most publishers wanted a share in publishing Scott, easily the most profitable author of the day, and some works were shared with Murray, Hurst, Robinson, Rees and Longman in London. John Murray of Albemarle Street, in whose rooms Scott and Byron met, started *The Quarterly Review* with Scott's assistance. After the financial crash Robert Cadell, Constable's young partner, became Scott's publisher. He was sharp, business-like and far-sighted. He persuaded Scott that a cheap collected edition of the Waverley Novels, with new Introductions by Scott, would help clear his debts. It was a revolutionary idea (originally Constable's brainwave) to sell the novels at a sixth of the old price and it began the process of creating the huge reading-public that was exploited throughout the nineteenth century by Dickens, Thackeray, Trollope, George Eliot and Hardy. When Scott died, Cadell made the best bargain of his life with Scott's elder son, in effect paying off the remainder of Scott's huge debt in return for the copyrights of the novels. He died a very wealthy man.

They are very like farmers, who thrive best at a high rent; and, in general, take most pains to sell a book that has cost them money to purchase.

Letters

I never wish to make a bargain by which the bookseller shall not have his full share of the advantage because the talent of writing and the power of selling books are two very different things.

Letters

I make it a rule to cheat nobody but Booksellers, a race on whom I have no mercy.

Letters

Look not thou on beauty's charming, –
Sit thou still when kings are arming, –
Taste not when the wine-cup glistens, –
Speak not when the people listens, –
Stop thine ear against the singer, –
From the red gold keep thy finger; –
Vacant heart and hand, and eye, –
Easy live and quiet die.

Lucy Ashton in *The Bride of Lammermoor*

— ON RAIN —

Here is a vile day, downright rain, which of course annihilates a part of the stock of human happiness. But what says the proverb of your true rainy day?

> Tis good for book, tis good for work
>   — For cup and can or knife and fork.

Journal

— ON RAPIDITY —

I believe no man now alive writes more rapidly than I do (no great recommendation), but I never think of making verses till I have a sufficient stock of poetical ideas to supply them.

Letters

To confess to you the truth, the works and passages in which I have succeeded have uniformly been written with the greatest rapidity.

The Fortunes of Nigel

The misfortune of writing fast is that one cannot at the same time write concisely.

Journal

— ON READING —

The purpose [of Constable's *Miscellany*] is to bring all the standard works both in science and the liberal arts within the reach of the lower classes and enable them thus to use with advantage the education which is given them at every hand. To make boys learn to read and then place no good books within their reach is to give men an appetite and leave nothing in the pantry save unwholesome and poisonous food which, depend upon it, they will eat rather than starve.

Journal

— ON REMOVALS —

A removal, or what we call a flitting, of all bores under the cope of heaven, is bore the most tremendous.

Letters

— ON RESPECT —

The mass of mankind will respect a monarch stained with actual guilt, more than one whose foibles render him only ridiculous.

The Fortunes of Nigel

— ON REVIEWING —

I do not at all like the task of reviewing and have seldom myself undertaken it – in poetry never – because I
am sensible there is a greater difference of tastes in that
department than in any other and that there is much
excellent poetry which I am not now-a-days able to
read without falling asleep.

Letters

— ON ROME —

Methinks I will not die quite happy without having
seen something of that Rome of which I have read
so much.

Letters

— ON SATIRE —

I have refrained as much as human frailty will permit from all satirical compositions.

Journal

— ON SAVING —

It is saving not getting that is the mother of Riches.

Journal

— ON SCHOOLMASTERS —

A schoolmaster has almost always something pedantic about him, from being long and constantly a man among boys.

Letters

O Caledonia, stern and wild,
Meet nurse for a poetic child!
Land of brown heath and shaggy wood,
Land of the mountain and the flood,
Land of my sires! What mortal hand
Can e'er untie the filial band
That knits me to thy rugged strand!

The Lay of the Last Minstrel

— ON SCOTTISH APPEARANCE —

His countenance was of the true Scottish cast, strongly marked, and rather harsh in features, with a shrewd and penetrating eye, and a countenance in which habitual gravity was enlivened by a cast of ironical humour.

The Antiquary

—ON SCOTTISH AUDIENCES —

Scottish audiences … are certainly not inclined to give applause upon credit.

Journal

— ON SCOTTISH CLANNISHNESS —

In Scotland men of all ranks but especially the middling and the lower classes are linked together by ties which give them a strong interest in each others' success in life and it is amazing the exertion which men will make to support and assist persons with whom you would suppose them connected by very remote ties of consanguinity and by no other link whatsoever.

Letters

— ON SCOTTISH GAIETY —

Assuredly Heaven did not form the Caledonian for the gay world; and his efforts at ease, grace, and gaiety resemble only the clumsy gambols of the ass in the fable.

Saint Ronan's Well

— ON SCOTTISH INDIVIDUALITY—

If you unscotch us you will find us damned mischievous Englishmen.

Letters

— SCOTTISH PROVERBIAL SAYINGS—

The hour's come but not the man.

Guy Mannering

My foot is on my native heath.

Rob Roy

There's a gude time coming.

Rob Roy

Better a finger off, as ay wagging.

Redgauntlet

It's ill speaking between a fou man and
a fasting.

Redgauntlet

The ae half of the warld thinks the tither daft.

Redgauntlet

It's ill taking the breeks aff a wild
Highlandman

The Fortunes of Nigel

— ON SCOTTISH SONGS —

The airs of our native country, imperfect as my musical
ear is, make and always have made the most pleasing
impression on me.

Journal

— ON SHAKESPEARE —

The blockheads talk of my being like Shakespeare – not
fit to tie his brogues.

Journal

SHAKESPEARE

A painting in the Shakespeare Centre in Stratford shows Scott standing bare-headed in front of the bust of Shakespeare in Holy Trinity church. Scott visited the Birthplace on two occasions; he knew some of Shakespeare's plays almost off by heart; he was a devoted supporter of Mrs Siddons and Edinburgh's Theatre Royal; he read Shakespeare aloud to his family, and he quoted him time after time in his letters and *Journal*. Those who compared Scott to Shakespeare were pooh-poohed by him but in one respect they were right. It was from Shakespeare's plays that he learned the art of welding together history and fiction. His and all succeeding historical novels owe much to the example of Shakespeare's history plays.

A hasty recollection will convince any of us how much better we are acquainted with those parts of English history which that immortal bard has dramatized than with any other portion of British story.

Peveril of the Peak

[*Holy Trinity Church, Stratford*] What a magic does the locality possess. There are stately monuments of forgotten families but when you have seen Shakespeare what care we for the rest?

Journal

The Commentators of Shakespeare have overburthened the text with notes and with disputes trivial in themselves and not always conducted with taste or temper.

Letters

— ON SOLDIERS —

I have a natural love for a soldier which would have been the mode of life I would have chosen in preference to all other but for my lameness.

Letters

— ON SPANIARDS —

A more inefficient yet a more resolved class of men than the Spaniards were never conceived.

Journal

— ON SPOUSES —

In gentle opposition like a well drilled spouse.

Letters

— ON STEAM-POWER —

The increasing powers of Steam which like you I look on 'half proud half sad, half angry and half pleased' in doing so much for the commercial world promise something also for the sociable, and like Prince Hossein's tapestry will I think one day waft friends together in the course of a few hours and for aught we may be able to tell bring Hampstead and Abbotsford within the distance of 'will you dine with us quietly to-morrow'.

Letters

Who knows how soon time and space may be actually abolished and Abbotsford be as near Saint Paul's as White Chapel.

Letters

— ON STOICISM —

Agere et pati Romanum est. Of all schools commend me to the Stoicks. We cannot indeed overcome our affections nor ought we if we could, but we can repress them within due bounds and avoid coaxing them to make fools of those who should be their masters.

Journal

I am a tolerable Stoic but preach to myself in vain.

Journal

— ON TARTAN —

I willingly give myself to be excited by the sight of handsome young men with plaids and claymores and all the alertness and spirit of highlanders in their native garb.

Journal

— ON TAX —

I am glad for one that ministers have lost their income tax – not that I have any particular objection to the tax itself which with a few more equitable modifications is perhaps as just as any or more so – but because it presented a tempting facility of raising money which was scarce to be trusted to any ministers excepting when the vital safety of the state is in danger.

Letters

TARTAN

How did the homespun checked cloth worn and woven in the wild Highland regions of Scotland become Scotland's national dress?

It was the King's visit in 1822 which started the tartan craze. Scott suggested that gentlemen should wear kilts (the dress at that time only of highlanders and the Edinburgh Celtic Society) and the King wore Highland Dress himself. Wilson's of Bannockburn seized the commercial opportunity and designed hundreds of supposed clan tartans. The fashion quickly spread abroad: a friend wrote to Scott in 1825 to say that 'tartan *à la Walter Scott*' was all the rage in Paris.

Nowadays around 5,000 designs are recorded in the official Scottish Register of Tartans.

The removing the taxes on tobacco and newspapers I look upon as a bonus to mental and physical poison.

Letters

— ON TEMPTATION —

Lord keep us from all temptation for we cannot be our own shepherd.

Journal

— ON TIPPING —

I own I like to pay postilions and waiters rather more liberally than perhaps is right. I hate grumbling and sour faces and the whole saving will not exceed a guinea or two for being cursed and damned from Dan to Beersheba.

Journal

— ON TRADITION —

If a church possessed the vessels out of which the original reformers partake of the Eucharist it would be surely bad taste to melt them down and exchange them for more modern. Law and Devotion must lose some of their dignity as often as they adopt new fashions.

Journal

— ON TRAVEL —

I am truly glad you are going abroad – nothing gives such a fillip to the imagination.

Letters

To see foreign parts gives I think more the feelings of youth to those of an advanced age than anything they can engage in.

Letters

Jock, when ye hae naething else to do, ye may be ay sticking in a tree; it will be growing, Jock, when ye're sleeping.

The Heart of Mid-Lothian

Planting and pruning trees I could work at from morning till night and if my poetical revenues enable me to have a few acres of my own that is one of the principle pleasures I look forward to. There is too a sort of self-congratulation, a little tickling self-flattery, in the idea that while you are pleasing and amusing yourself you are really seriously contributing to the future welfare of the country and that your very acorn may send its ribs of oak to future victories like Trafalgar.

Letters

There's naething sae gude on this side o' time but it might hae been better, and that may be said o' the Union. Nane were keener against it than the Glasgow folk, wi' their rabblings and their risings, and their mobs, as they ca' them nowadays. But it's an ill wind blaws naebody gude. I say, Let Glasgow flourish! Whilk is judiciously and elegantly putten round the town's arms, by way of by-word – Now, since Saint Mungo catched herrings in the Clyde, what was ever like to gar us flourish like the sugar and tobacco-trade? Will ony body tell me that, and grumble at the treaty that opened us a road west-awa yonder?

Bailie Nicol Jarvie in *Rob Roy*

When we had a king, and a chancellor, and parliament-men o' our ain, we could aye peeble them wi'stanes when they werena gude bairns – but naebody's nails can reach the length o'Lunnon.

Mrs Howden in The Heart of Mid-Lothian

The mail-coach and the Berwick smacks have done more than the Union in altering our national char-acter, sometimes for the better and sometimes for the worse.

Letters

— ON THE UNITIES —

The unities of time and place have always appeared to me fopperies, as far as they require close observance of the French rules. Still, the nearer you can come to them, it is always, no doubt, the better, because your action will be more probable. But the unity of action – I mean that continuity which unites every scene with the other, and makes the catastrophe the natural and prob-able result of all that has gone before – seems to me a critical rule which cannot safely be dispensed with.

Letters

— ON VICTORIA —

I was presented to the little Princess Victoria, I hope they will change her name, the heir apparent to the crown as things now stand. She is fair like the royal family but does not look as if she would be pretty.

Journal

— ON VIOLIN MUSIC —

I do not understand or care about fine music but there is something in [Sandy Ballantyne's] violin which goes to the very heart.

Journal

— ON VISITORS —

In came Colonel Fergusson with Mrs. Stewart of Blackhill or hall or something, and I must show her the garden, pictures etc. This lasts till one, and just as they are at their lunch and obliged to go off, guard is relieved

by the Laird and Lady Harden and Miss Eliza Scott;
and my dear chief whom I love very much though he
is a little obsidional or so remains till three. That same
crown composed of the grass which grew on the walls
of besieged places should be offered to visitors who
stay above an hour in any decent person's house.

Journal

— ON VOLUMINOUS AUTHORS —

It is some consolation to reflect, that the best authors
in all countries have been the most voluminous.

The Fortunes of Nigel

— ON JAMES WATT —

Men like Watt whose genius tends strongly to invent and execute those wonderful combinations which extend in such an incalculable degree the human force and command over the physical world do not come within ordinary rules.

Letters

— ON WEATHER —

If a man relaxed the custom of his exercise in Scotland for a bad day he is not like to resume it in a hurry.

Journal

Frank Osbaldistone: Fine weather for your work, my friend
Andrew Fairservice: It's no that muckle to be compleened of.

Rob Roy

If there's a fair day in seven, Sunday's sure to come and lick it up.

Andrew Fairservice in Rob Roy

— ON WELLINGTON —

In fact my trust is and has long been in that one man who possesses in a higher degree the gift of common sense than in anyone I have heard or read of. He is the only Man of whom I could say like Robert Bruce to the Lord of the Isles 'My trust is constant in thee'.

Letters

I had to-day a most kind and friendly letter from the Duke of Wellington, which is a thing to be vain of. He is a wonderful man to have climbed to such a height without ever slipping his foot. Who would have said in 1815 that the Duke would stand still higher in 1829? And yet it indubitably is so.

Journal

— ON WINE —

A glass of good wine is a gracious creature and reconciles poor mortality to itself, and that is what few things can do.

Journal

Without being a veteran Vice, a Grey Iniquity, like Falstaff, I think an occasional jolly bout if not carried to excess improved society. Men were put into good humour 'when the good wine did its good office'; the jest, the song, the speech had double effect; men were happy for the night and better friends ever after because they had been so.

Journal

Wine unveils the passions and throws away restraint but it does not create habits or opinions which did not previously exist in the mind.

Letters

Depend upon it, of all vices drinking is the most incompatible with greatness.

Lockhart's *Life of Scott*

— ON WOMEN —

O, Woman! in our hours of ease,
Uncertain, coy, and hard to please,
And variable as the shade
By the light quivering aspen made;
When pain and anguish wring the brow,
A ministering angel thou!

Marmion

WOMEN

Scott did not marry his first love, Williamina Belsches, who preferred the wealthy banker William Forbes to the impecunious lawyer and poet. However his marriage to Charlotte Carpenter, a Frenchwoman whose French accent and pride in her barouche landau did not endear her to everyone in Edinburgh, seems to have been happy. They had two sons and two daughters. Scott was fond of both girls. Sophia, who was maternal, hypochondriac and married to John Gibson Lockhart (later Scott's biographer), delighted him by singing Scots songs to the accompaniment of her harp. Her witty and vivacious younger sister Anne became his housekeeper and companion after Charlotte's death.

There were no love affairs outside the marriage but Scott liked the company of intelligent women and had many female friends and correspondents.

Fair, fat and forty.

Saint Ronan's Well

Woman's faith, and woman's trust –
Write the characters in dust.

The Betrothed

I hate having to deal with ladies when they are in an unreasonable humour.

Journal

I do believe your destitute widow, especially if she hath a charge of children and one or two fit for patronage, is one of the most impudent animals living.

Journal

— ON WOMEN NOVELISTS —

The Big Bow wow strain I can do myself like any now going but the exquisite touch which renders ordinary common-place things and characters interesting from the truth of the description and the sentiment is denied to me.

The women do this better – Edgeworth, Ferrier, Austen have all had their portraits of real society far superior to anything Man vain Man has produced of the like nature.

Journal

— ON WORDSWORTH —

Wordsworth in particular is such a character as only exists in romance – virtuous, simple, and unaffectedly restricting every want and wish to the bounds of a very narrow income in order to enjoy the literary and poetical leisure in which his happiness consists.

Letters

WORDSWORTH

The last visitors to Abbotsford in 1831 before Scott sailed to the Mediterranean in a vain attempt to regain his health were Wordsworth and his daughter. Scott and Wordsworth had been friends for nearly thirty years, ever since the poet called at Scott's cottage in Lasswade so early in the morning that the family were not yet up. They met in London and the Lake District, where they climbed Helvellyn together and both wrote a poem about it. It distressed Scott that Wordsworth would not make money by writing popular narrative poems like his, and it amused John Lockhart, Scott's son-in-law, that when they were together Scott would often quote Wordsworth but that Wordsworth never returned the compliment. Scott shared Wordsworth's love of rugged countryside and approved of his manly common sense, so different from the affectation of many literary men which he heartily disliked.

Wordsworth is a man and a gentleman every inch of him unless when he is mounted on his critical hobby horse and tells one Pope is no poet. He might as well say Wellington is no soldier because he wears a blue great coat and not a coat of burnished mail.

Letters

I do not at all acquiesce in his system of poetry and I think he has injured his own fame by adhering to it. But a better or more sensible man I do not know than W.W.

Journal

— ON WRITING —

No man of sense in any rank of life is, or ought to be, above accepting a just recompense for his time, and a reasonable share of the capital which owes its very existence to his exertions. No man of honour, genius, or spirit, would make the mere love of gain the chief, far less the only, purpose of his labours. For myself, I am not displeased to find the game a winning one; yet, while I pleased the public, I should probably continue it merely for the pleasure of playing; for I have felt as strongly as most folks the love of composition which is perhaps the strongest of all instincts.

The Fortunes of Nigel

A thing may already be so well told in history that Romance ought not in prudence to meddle with it.

Journal

Where historical characters are introduced it ought only to be incidentally and in such a manner as not to interfere with established truth.

Letters

After all works of fiction, viz. Cursed Lies, are easier to write and much more popular than the best truths.

Journal

In general I think it ungentlemanly to wound any person's feelings through an anonymous publication unless where conceit or false doctrine strongly calls for reprobation.

Letters

A man of business, even a lawyer, does not take any advantage from literary acquirements; they are on the contrary sometimes supposed to divert him from his professional pursuits and so far the reputation of possessing them is a positive disadvantage. To live the life of a mere author for bread is perhaps the most dreadful fate that can be encountered.

Letters

I am persuaded both children and the lower class of readers hate books which are written down to their capacity and love those that are more composed for their elders and betters.

Journal

Those who do not work from necessity take violent labour from choice and were necessity out of the question I would take the same sort of literary labour from choice.

Journal

— ON YODELLING —

I cannot but think that their udalling, if this be the word, is a variation or set of variations upon the tones of a jackass.

Journal